D0975441

REMEMBERING *for* BOTH OF US

A Child Learns about Alzheimer's

By Charlotte Wood
Illustrations by Dennis Auth

ISBN: 978-1-9399303-8-5

Library of Congress Control Number: 2014949914

Brandylane

BRANDYLANEPUBLISHERS.COM

ACKNOWLEDGMENTS

My special thanks to my children and especially to my dear grandchildren, Imani, Jaylen, and Faith, who provided inspiration for the book; and to my sister, brothers, nieces, nephews, and their families for their understanding and support.

My great appreciation to Charlie and Thomas for their invaluable work of reading, editing, and helping in any way needed until the book's completion.

My heartfelt thanks to my husband's medical team and caregivers for their care and the many friends and acquaintances, and even strangers who, when told the purpose of the book, offered well-wishing words of encouragement.

My most sincere thanks to Robert Pruett of Brandylane Publishers for understanding the book's significance and for his commitment, along with that of illustrator Dennis Auth, in making *Remembering for Both of Us* a reality.

Finally, to Charles Burnett III, my immeasurable gratitude for his role in making this book possible.

May God be praised for His infinite love and help in time of need.

I dedicate this book in memory of my beloved husband, Bill, who for many years bravely battled the devastating illness of Alzheimer's. And to my family and all families, especially the children and grandchildren, who struggle to understand and deal with the impact of this baffling disease.

"Love is patient, love is kind . . . Love never fails."

1 Corinthians 13:4–8

Tasha's grandfather loved it whenever Tasha came to visit. He would wait for her on the front lawn, and before her mother's car could even stop, he would excitedly call to Grandmom, "Honey, they're here!"

"Precious Little Girl" was the name he had lovingly given his first grandchild when he held her for the first time. Now he would rush to greet her, sometimes with candy, toys or other treats.

Precious Little Girl was happy to see her PaPa, too. They always did fun and exciting things together.

Grandmom and PaPa were very happy to take care of Tasha while her parents were at work. They enjoyed helping Tasha and seeing her grow and learn. They saw her take her first steps!

Her grandparents taught her lots of things: how to put on her shoes and tie the laces; to wash her hands and say grace before eating; to eat her vegetables and drink milk because it would make her healthy. And of course they taught her to say "please" and "thank you" and to always be kind to others.

Tasha learned quickly, but sometimes she forgot. PaPa told her to always wait for him before feeding the cat. One day she tried to do it herself—and milk spilled everywhere! But PaPa and Grandmom were patient, and explained again why it was important to pay attention and listen carefully to them.

No one had to tell Tasha to pay attention when PaPa opened up his big red tool box.

Tasha would ask:

"What is that?"
"What does it do?"
"What's that funny-looking thing?"

As PaPa looked through his many shiny and oddly shaped tools, he would patiently stop to answer her questions. "You need the right tool to fix something right," he would often say. And when he allowed her to hold or hand him something, she was so proud.

PaPa loved working on projects and fixing things. Sometimes Tasha would help or watch him from a safe distance. He built and painted birdhouses. Sometimes he worked under the hood of his van, whistling while his tools clinked.

PaPa also took Grandmom and Tasha on many trips in the van. He told them jokes and stories. Talking, laughing and singing made the trips special.

PaPa and Precious Little Girl always had a special relationship. But as time passed, some things changed. Tasha now had a little brother and baby sister. And when Tasha was ten years old, her grandparents moved to a new house across town. She missed them picking her up from day care and taking her home. Now she took the bus. Tasha was getting used to these changes, but there was something else changing that she did not understand, and this troubled her. *PaPa was changing.*

Now when Tasha and her family visited her grandparents, it was Grandmom who called out "Look who's here!". . . not PaPa. Instead, he looked sad or confused. He didn't do fun things with Tasha any more. He asked questions over and over. He once put his keys in the refrigerator, and another time, he poured milk into the sugar bowl. One day he even put his shoes on the wrong feet.

Tasha noticed Grandmom looking out for PaPa as he had once done for Tasha.

Grandmom would patiently answer his questions. She would tell him how to do things, what to do and what not to do:

"That's not your coat, honey."
"Close the door behind you."
"Turn off the water in the sink."

When Tasha asked her parents what was happening to PaPa, they didn't seem to want to talk about it. But Tasha could tell that they were worried, too. Why did Grandmom look so upset when PaPa forgot things? Why was PaPa so irritable? She didn't understand what was happening to PaPa—not one bit!

At breakfast one day, Tasha's mother said she had good news to share: "PaPa is going to an adult day care center!"

Tasha's little brother giggled and said, "PaPa's going to a day care like me?"

Before Tasha could ask *why*, her dad explained, "It's a day care for grown-ups. PaPa will have fun there like you do at your day care."

"May I stay with Grandmom while PaPa is at adult day care on my next school break?" Tasha quickly asked. "I can keep her company while he's gone."

"That's a great idea!" her dad said.

On the day Tasha came, Grandmom greeted her with a big hug, but PaPa didn't. He didn't say "Hello, Precious Little Girl!" He just sat silently in his chair.

When it was time to go to the adult day care center, Grandmom had to help PaPa get ready. "Put on your cap," she told him. "Here is your jacket. Whoops, wrong arm . . . "

When they got into the car, Grandmom drove. PaPa asked where they were going over and over. Grandmom answered patiently. She reminded him of all the fun he would have with his friends.

Still, no matter what Grandmom said, PaPa seemed upset. Leaving PaPa at the day care was not easy.

"Have fun. Enjoy your friends!" Grandmom said. "We'll be back after lunch." Grandmom tried to sound cheerful. But Tasha could tell she was nervous because PaPa looked so unhappy.

On the ride home, both Tasha and Grandmom were quiet. There was none of the talk and laughter that Tasha used to look forward to. They just listened to quiet music on the radio. Sometimes, Grandmom tried to hum along.

What was happening to PaPa?

Tasha wondered how she could get the answers she wanted, as Grandmom wondered how she could better explain it all to Tasha . . .

When they got home, Tasha and Grandmom said, almost at the same time, "Now what can we do?" Seeing their little gray cat waiting for them helped brighten their mood.

Grandmom had an idea. "Let's work on that scrapbook you got for your birthday."

It didn't take long to find it in the back room. They also found a craft box filled with glue and scissors and all the supplies they needed.

"And look, Tasha," said Grandmom. "Here's a bag of PaPa's favorite peppermints. They can be our treat while we work."

Grandmom and Tasha sat down and began going through the family pictures. The pictures reminded them of all the fun things they had done as a family.

Tasha was full of questions:

"Is that really me as a baby?"
"Who is that?"
"Where are we in this picture?"
"Remember this?"
"What an exciting day that was!"

Looking at the pictures and talking about the fun times made the sad feelings disappear. Then Tasha found a picture of herself and PaPa standing in front of a brick building. It was a picture of her first day of day care. The picture reminded Tasha of dropping PaPa off at the adult day care center.

Tasha turned to Grandmom and asked, "What's *really* happening to PaPa?"

Grandmom was grateful for the chance to talk seriously to Tasha about PaPa. This was the moment both of them had been waiting for.

Grandmom took Tasha's hand. She said, "PaPa has something called Alzheimer's."

"Alls-hime-ers," Tasha tried to say the word. "What's that?"

"It's the name of a disease that some adults get when they grow older. It's a disease that makes you lose your memory," Grandmom answered. "At first you forget everyday things, like combing your hair or turning off the faucet. Then you begin to forget how to do things, even things you once enjoyed doing and did well. You stop recognizing the people you love. They become like strangers to you . . . and that's very frightening."

Tasha thought about it. She tried hard to imagine what it would be like not to know anyone or how to do anything. She looked at the picture again and remembered her first day at day care. She had not known how to do the things her teacher had wanted her to do. At first, she had not even known who the other kids were, or where anything was. She remembered how scary that had been. She wondered if that was how PaPa felt now.

"Can doctors make him better?" Tasha asked Grandmom.

"Well, there are medicines that help. And going to adult day care helps him because PaPa gets to exercise, to be active and get help from people trained to work with Alzheimer's patients. But there is no cure . . . yet."

As Grandmom said this, it looked as if she might cry.

"Is there anything I can do to help?" Tasha asked, patting Grandmom on the shoulder.

Grandmom began to smile. "Of course. Maybe you can help him with something he has forgotten how to do, or work on crafts with him. These are ways to show how much you love him, Tasha."

Tasha nodded. She was beginning to understand what was happening to PaPa and what she could do to help him.

They kept working on Tasha's scrapbook, picking out their favorite photos and gluing them to the pages. Tasha decorated the pages with colored markers. Lastly, she drew a red heart in the corner of each page.

Soon, it was time to pick up PaPa. Tasha slipped something into her pocket as they were leaving.

When they saw PaPa, Tasha ran to him and gave him a big hug. Then she reached into her pocket and pulled out the peppermint candy she had brought.

"PaPa, here's a treat for you." She handed him the peppermint candy.

PaPa took it, unwrapped it, popped it into his mouth, and said, "Thank you, Precious Little Girl." He was smiling now and seemed happy to see Tasha and Grandmom.

At that moment, one of the caregivers asked Papa to show them what he had done during craft time. Papa hesitated at first, but then proudly held up a scrapbook page he had decorated. Grandmom and Tasha could hardly believe their eyes.

"PaPa, that design you made is just like the ones we did today," said Tasha. Grandmom agreed. The colors were the same, and each corner had pretty red hearts. Everyone was amazed and happy at what had just happened.

Knowing more about what was happening to PaPa made Tasha want to show him even more love and attention. However, Grandmom could still see sadness in Tasha's eyes whenever she visited. When Tasha spoke to PaPa, he would look at her, but usually, he would say nothing. How could Grandmom help her grandchild understand that while PaPa was changing, his love for Tasha had not?

The answer she had been praying for came to Grandmom one weekend as she and Tasha were preparing their favorite pancake breakfast. She thanked Tasha for being extra kind to PaPa and for setting a good example for her brother and sister.

"Tasha," Grandmom said, "remember how your PaPa always used to call you 'Precious Little Girl?' Well, whenever you see PaPa now, just imagine him saying 'Hello, Precious Little Girl' to you. You know that's what he would say—if he could. Will you remember that?"

A smile lit up Tasha's face. She quickly went over to the chair where her PaPa sat sleeping. Looking at him with love, she whispered, "Yes, PaPa, I'll remember . . . I'll remember for both of us!"

A Word About Alzheimer's Disease

Some experts believe that as many as 5.1 million Americans may already have Alzheimer's. This disease slowly destroys memory and thinking skills. The number is expected to continue to grow in years to come. Numerous research projects are being conducted to find causes and ways to detect, prevent and hopefully cure this baffling and devastating disease. In the meantime, many victims and their families must cope with its many difficult challenges.

My sincere desire is that as this story is read, it will in some way give insight, encouragement and hope to young readers and their families, who are confronting similar conditions created by their family members' struggle with Alzheimer's. And remember, September is World Alzheimer's Awareness Month.

Learn More about Alzheimer's:

Contact:
National Alzheimer's Association
1-800-272-3900
www.alz.org

About the Author

Charlotte B. Wood retired after thirty-two years of teaching in the Chesterfield, Virginia, public schools. The birth of her first grandchild provided Charlotte with the inspiration to pursue her hobby of writing for children. Sadly, her husband, William, also a teacher, was diagnosed with Alzheimer's shortly after his retirement; he passed in 2013. Charlotte's desire to share insights learned from the challenges of her husband's illness resulted in *Remembering for Both of Us*. Hopefully, this will enable children and others to better understand this baffling disease. She resides in Midlothian, Virginia, and is active in her community and church.

About the Illustrator

Dennis Auth hails from Pittsburgh, Pennsylvania, where teaching guitar and leading a rock band landed him in art school, inspiring instructors and fellow design students alike. He began freelancing after relocating as an ad-agency art director to Virginia Beach, where he illustrated in multiple media for projects ranging from children's books to striking architecture.

The Tidewater area is home to Dennis, his wife, and their grown children.